## More Advance Praise for
### *The Sound of Shadows*

Chase Gagnon is a writer who edges his work with atmosphere: Even haiku, in its incredible briefness, can be a poem made larger by the storyteller's gift. As haiku is such a brief approach to writing poetry it could be said, paraphrasing Chase's words, to be firefly ghosts in a frosted mason jar in moonlight. He is very much an up and coming writer creating excitement amongst writers and readers. His work is a breeze of shadows; a gypsy's finger-cymbals pinching the stars; but oh how slowly the fireflies disappear while he slides his lips across the harmonica. – Alan Summers, Founder of With Words


'lonely night
I slide my lips across
the harmonica'

An old spirit in the body of a young man. Chase Gagnon's feelings run deep and strong. Spoken from the soul of a sage, 'The Sound of Shadows' will help you remember how to feel. – Sandi Pray, poet

# The Sound of Shadows

by Chase Gagnon

Mijikai Press
Raleigh, North Carolina
2014

The Sound of Shadows

Copyright © 2014 by Chase Gagnon

All rights reserved. This book or any portion thereof may not be reproduced or used in any manner whatsoever without the express written permission of the author except for the use of brief quotations in a book review.

First Printing, 2014
ISBN-13: 978-1501072970
Published by
Mijikai Press
2901 Old Orchard Road
Raleigh, NC 27607

www.facebook.com/MijikaiPress

Dedicated to Helen Buckingham, Collin Barber, and Julie Warther.

first chill...
a lily awakens to
the sound of shadows


I dig a moat
for a forgotten sandcastle...
morning drizzle

predawn dew
the chill of darkness
between my toes


waking from a dream...
the humpback's tail slips down
into the sea


morning moon —
a stranger's scent
in my bed

cemetery sunrise...
the old padlocked gate
shudders in wind


breathless
in the chill of dawn
a winter birdsong

last star
the weight of snowflakes
on my lashes


no turning back
morning blushes
in our whispers


scattering your ashes
the morning tide
still pulled by the moon

asleep on the curb
a gentle rain
tapping his bongos


shoreside grave:
continents of fog
adrift on the lake

no one's footsteps
left to follow —
late winter rain


forgotten battlefield...
a crash of thunder
shakes the grass


end of summer
my henna tattoo
turning orange

church bells at dusk
how slowly the fireflies
disappear


twilight drizzle...
raindrops cling to the clothesline
in a breeze of shadows

darkening sunset...
I watch a mosquito fill
with my blood


talk of past lives
the slow pulse
of a firefly in my palm


darkening twilight —
will this mayfly
outlive me?

lonely night
I slide my lips
across the harmonica


chilly dusk
the taste of dark chocolate
in her kiss

desert motel
darkness nestles
into an empty cow skull


graveyard raven...
my shadow shackled
around my ankles


desert junkyard...
in an old chevy's mirror
a million stars

ancient songs...
an elder's sweat rolls
off the bone-flute


skylight moon...
how thin the veil
of my wildest dreams

invisible
to my lover, in the dark...
midnight thunder


her ashes settle
in the pond...
starry night


humid night
a tadpole breaks the surface
of ancient stars

fade of midnight rain
reawakening the song
of crickets



a dark lighthouse
hangs over the moonlit sea...
unspoken love

firefly ghosts
in the frosted mason jar...
harvest moonlight


tethered to the call
of the midnight owl;
I dangle over a dream


last embers
falling from the incense...
end of autumn

moonless night
a gypsy's finger-cymbals
pinch the stars


christmas eve
the beggar's palm fills
with snowflakes

## Acknowledgements

The following poems were published previously in the journals indicated:

"no one's footsteps" – A Hundred Gourds 3:4
"end of summer" – Modern Haiku 45.2
"predawn dew" – Shamrock 28
"waking from a dream"... -- AGH 2:3, 2013 Red Moon Anthology "fear of Dancing"
"lonely night" – A Hundred Gourds 3:2
"scattering your ashes" – A Hundred Gourds 3:4
"last star" -- Cattails, may 2014, youth corner section
"humid night" – 2nd place in Sharpening the Green Pencil haiku contest 2014
"firefly ghosts" – A Hundred Gourds 3:2
"last embers" -- Editor's Choice, Cattails Premier Edition
"moonless night"... -- Under the Basho 2014

Chase Gagnon is a student who lives in Michigan. *The Sound of Shadows* is his first poetry chapbook

Made in the USA
Charleston, SC
28 September 2014